PYROGRAPHY FOR BEGINNERS

The Quick-Start Guide to Getting Started in Woodburning, with Basics on Tools, Tips, Tricks, and Techniques, and Safety, to Create Beautiful Art and Gifts Easily

ALEXIA SANSONE

Copyright @2022

COPYRIGHT @2022 ALEXIA SANSONE

All rights reserved. No parts of this book may be reproduced, transmitted in any form or by any means – mechanical, electronic, photocopy, recording or any other except for brief quotations in printed reviews, without prior permission of the publisher.

Table of Contents

CHAPTER ONE 1

INTRODUCTION 1

What is Pyrography? 1

Wood Burning History 2

CHAPTER TWO 5

THE REQUIRED SUPPLIES 5

Wood Burning Pen Tool 6

No Temperature Control vs. Temperature Control 10

The Different Burning Tips 11

Choosing a Wood burning Tool 13

Solid-Point Burners 14

Wire-Nib Burners 15

Pros and the Cons of the Burners 16

How to Use the wood Burning Tool 20

The Wood 22

Selecting the Wood 25
CHAPTER THREE 29
OTHER WOOD BURNING TOOLS 29
The Necessary Tools 29
The Not-So-Necessary Tools 41
CHAPTER FOUR 43
WOOD BURNING PROCEDURE 43
Preparing Your Wood 43
Selecting Your Design 45
Burning Your Design 49
Adding Color to Your Art 52
Finishing Your Pyrography Art 53
Tips on Making Your First Project Successful 54
Tips on the Tips 54
Tips While You're Working 56
Tips for Finishing the Piece 59

CHAPTER FIVE 61
  PYROGRAPHY STENCILS 61
    Premade Stencils 62
    Graphite Paper 65
    Carbon Paper 69
    Patterns and Designs Selection 71
    Start Working on Your Project 74
CHAPTER SIX 76
  TECHNIQUES AND TRICKS 76
    Basic Outlines 76
    Filling Silhouettes (Technique) 77
    Gradient Effect (Technique) 78
    Hatching (Technique) 80
    Textures (Technique) 81
    Background Techniques 83
CHAPTER SEVEN 89
  CLEANING PYROGRAPHY TOOL TIPS 89

The Most Effective Cleaning Methods 90
   Leather Strop and Aluminum Oxide............................ 91
   Honing Cleaning Cloth 93
Acceptable Cleaning Methods 94
   Razor Blade or Knife 94
   Brass Bristled Brush........ 96
   Steel Wool or Scouring Pad 97
   Tea Strainer 99
Awful Cleaning Methods ... 101
   Sandpaper and Sanding Blocks......................... 102
   Emery Boards and Files . 103
   Wet Sponge.................. 104
CHAPTER EIGHT 105
PYROGRAPHY SAFETY GEAR, TIPS AND TRICKS.............. 105
   Safety Tools and Gear 105

Safety Tips and Tricks 107
Worst Woods for Pyrography
.... 110
Best woods for Pyrography 114
CHAPTER NINE 116
BEGINNER SAMPLE PATTERNS
.... 116
CHAPTER TEN 120
IN CONCLUSION 120

CHAPTER ONE
INTRODUCTION

What is Pyrography?

Pyrography is a technique for decorating wood or leather by burning a design into the surface with heat. I'll be concentrating on pyrography as wood burning in this guide.

Pyrography can be used to decorate a wide range of wooden items, including dinnerware (for example, spoons, plates, and bowls), kitchenware (for example, cutting boards), and general home decor (such as boxes, chests).

There are only a few supplies required, and the majority of them may be obtained in a handy beginner's kit! Wood and a wood burning pen are the two most important items to have on hand for sketching designs onto the surface.

Wood Burning History

Pyrography, also known as wood burning, is a centuries-old technique that dates back to almost the moment humanity discovered fire. Humans understood that, after fire was discovered, it could be used to burn symbols and pictograms into wood.

During the Middle Ages, it was common for blacksmiths to dabble in pyrography as well. Because blacksmiths routinely utilized heated metal, they learned that the hot metal could also be used to burn elaborate artwork onto other surfaces. This type of wood burning was commonly employed to embellish chests and containers.

As the art of wood burning progressed, the instruments employed in the craft evolved as well. To make things easier for pyrography artists, smaller tools that could be grasped like writing utensils were created. These wood burning pens make learning and enjoying this pastime much easier for artisan crafters.

CHAPTER TWO

THE REQUIRED SUPPLIES

Before you start wood burning, you'll need a few important tools. All of the essential tools can usually be found in a beginner's pyrography kit at your local craft store or online. Before investing in more serious instruments, I would recommend starting with one of those wood burning for beginners' kits. If you wish to pursue this activity further, you should be aware of the various types of wood burning instruments available.

The following are the basic tools and supplies you'll need to begin wood burning:

- ✓ Wood burning pen
- ✓ Wood
- ✓ Carbon or Graphite paper
- ✓ Ruler
- ✓ Masking tape, artist's tape, or painter's tape
- ✓ Mineral or olive oil (applied on the finished work)
- ✓ Eraser
- ✓ Sandpaper
- ✓ Printed design

You won't need paper, printed designs, or tape if you utilize a physical stencil.

Wood Burning Pen Tool

The design of a wood-burning pen or wood burner is similar to that of a soldering iron. The best pens have heat-resistant handles, which are meant to stay cool as you hold the tool.

A metal element in the pen heats up. Depending on the lines and designs you choose, you can customize your pen by attaching different tips to it.

The wood burner includes certain safety precautions because you're working with equipment that gets incredibly hot. The pen features a barrier between the handle and the metal to save your fingers from getting burned while you're working.

Wood burners additionally come with a metal stand that you use to keep the tool from scorching your work surface and causing a fire danger.

Wood pens are available for purchase online, at hobby stores, and in woodworking shops. They're not hard to get by. They're frequently sold in packages that include many tips as well as other items like stencils.

You hold the wood burner in the same way you would a standard pen or pencil to utilize it. To avoid burning your fingers, you must keep them above the guard. As you become more familiar with the tool, you will discover the grip that is most comfortable for you.

The cost of a wood burner can range from around $20 to hundreds of dollars. The cheapest models usually don't have a temperature control, so you can only turn them on and off. You have no control over the temperature (i.e., heat).

The other choice is a temperature-control option, which allows you to precisely control the burning temperature. They'll set you back a little more, with the most affordable options costing around $40.

No Temperature Control vs. Temperature Control

No Temperature Control	Temperature Control
Extremely affordable	More expensive
One temperature necessitates more competence	Greater control over the burn
Requires considerable trial and error	Simpler for a novice to utilize

Most experts think that if you're going to spend a bit extra on a pen, you should spend it on temperature control. With softwood, it's simpler to learn how hot the pen is, and the craft.

The Different Burning Tips

In pyrography, the tips that come with your wood burner or those you purchase separately play a critical role.

The tips are what enable you to draw various lines and patterns on the wood.

Your wood-burning pen's tip screws or snaps into the end. They're always made of metal, and each one has a unique design or shape. Certain tips will even burn letters, similar to a brand, which simplifies the process of creating letters.

These are some of the most prevalent tips and their use:

Name of Tip	Use
Calligraphy	Writing, fine lines
Universal	A range of lines
Dot	Holes, dots, fine lines
Branding	Specific patterns depending on the design of the tip
Groove	Grooves and gouges
Shading	Branding or shading a teardrop

Choosing a Wood burning Tool

It is up to you, choosing the best wood burning tool.

- ✓ What is the state of your patience?
- ✓ Are you willing to put in more time or spend more money?
- ✓ How does this affect your bank account?
- ✓ Are you even aware of the appropriate questions to ask?

Here are the two primary types of wood burning machines, or "models":

- ✓ Solid-Point, and
- ✓ Wire-Nib

Solid-Point Burners

A solid-point tool resembles a soldering iron in appearance (it IS a soldering iron 99.9 percent of the time).

Beginners may find it difficult to figure out how to get this tool to burn nicely. It gets the job done, but it lacks the comfort of a new and automatic tool.

While some expert artists prefer solid point machines, the majority of pyrographers opt for the sleeker wire-nib types.

Solid-point machines have these features:

- ✓ For novices, useful but not necessarily easy
- ✓ Won't eat a hole in your bank
- ✓ On several levels, however, it is clumsy and slow

Wire-Nib Burners

The wire-nibbed pyrography pens resemble real "pens" far more than the solid point wood burners.

They're a lot more fun to use than solid points, and they're a lot easier to learn how to use.

Wire-nib machines are usually:

- ✓ Faster
- ✓ Easier
- ✓ More potent

✓ However, they have a tendency to eat a hole in your cash reserve.

Pros and the Cons of the Burners

Who they are for:

Solid-Point	Wire-Nib
Suitable for beginners on a budget of less than $50	Suitable for beginners with budget of $100 and/or more
Acceptable for advanced artists, but limited	Excellent for skilled artists interested in taking their woodburning to the next level

Excellent for artists of all skill levels who have a lot of time to work on things (because a lot of patience is required)	Excellent for artists of all ability levels who wish to work more quickly

The pros:

Solid-Point	Wire-Nib
Cheaper	Handle is thinner, more akin to a pen
Small and convenient to carry or store	Rapid heating and cooling

	Increased control over the temperature (heat)
	There are more nib/point options
	The machine is attached to the stand

The cons:

Solid-Point	Wire-Nib
Handle is thick, hefty, and awkward (difficult to hold)	More expensive

The tips/points are more difficult to use	Has a large machine that is difficult to transport and store
Heats up and cools down slowly	
Heat controls are limited	
Styles of tip/point are limited	
The stand must be securely fastened to the table	

How to Use the wood Burning Tool

1. Go over the entire set of instructions included with your tool.

2. Check that your wood burning tool is turned off (, or unplugged) and cooled.

3. Screw on, cnto the wood burner, the desired tip.

4. Allow the wood burning equipment at least 5 minutes to heat up after plugging it in.

5. To begin burning in your design, gently place the tip onto the wood's surface. To

burn even colored lines, keep the pressure steady (, or constant). Avoid excessive pressure while creating darker lines to avoid damaging the nib. Instead, leave the nib in the same spot until the desired shade is achieved.

6. Lift the wood burning tool off the wood once you've finished sketching in a line or shape. It's possible that allowing it to remain on the wood surface will result in a burn spot.

7. Before touching the tip of the wood burner to change the

nibs, ensure it is unplugged and cooled down. To avoid damage, keep nibs in an enclosed case. If the nibs are still hot, you can use needle-nose pliers to remove them.

8. While wearing gloves, use sandpaper to lightly clean the wood burner nib. Wipe the nib clean with a soft cloth. This is to guarantee that no wood residue remains on the nib, dulling it.

The Wood

This activity requires the use of wood. You'd have nothing to burn if it weren't for it! Pyrography can be done on soft woods, although some artists choose woods that are a little more durable, such as pine, basswood, birch, or bamboo. Elm and oak are hardwoods that may also be used, but they are usually reserved for more skilled artists.

- ✓ Pine — Low-cost, but with uneven grains
- ✓ Birch — Light burning, and with a smooth surface
- ✓ Basswood — Light burning wood with a smooth surface and uniform grains
- ✓ Bamboo — Smooth and inexpensive material

- ✓ Oak — Moisture in wood, and uneven grains
- ✓ Poplar — Soft grains, burns easily, and can be costly
- ✓ Cedar wood — Soft wood with grains that are not troublesome. Gradient shadings will be scarcely visible, while line art will stand out nicely
- ✓ Cherry wood — Smells great while you're working

Burning straight lines can be difficult due to uneven grains in the wood. Beginners should stick to wood that has a smooth surface and even grain. More high-quality wood, on the other hand, can be costly. Beginner wood burners may want to use pine because it is affordable and widely available. However, it's crucial not to get disheartened because the quality of the wood can affect the outcome of your art.

Never burn wood that has been treated in any way. Burning varnish is bad for your health, and it can even cause the wood to burst into little flames.

Selecting the Wood

Before you begin your woodworking project, the next step is to select your wood. Any sort of wood can be used, but some are preferable for beginners than others.

I. You should aim for soft wood with little grain. A light-colored wood is preferable since it will allow the burning to show up more clearly, but a darker wood will make it more difficult to notice your artwork. Poplar, birchwood, and basswood are the best options.

II. Hardwood can be used, although it is more difficult to burn and requires more heat. When dealing with hard wood, you can expect to spend more time than when working with soft wood. This might not be the best wood for a beginner.

III. You can also use waste wood, but avoid using wood that has been treated with a finish. When you start burning, this poses a health risk.

Because you'll need a fresh piece for each job, this will most likely be the most expensive supply you'll require. You might be able to gather wood for free in nature or get scrap pieces from a lumber yard for a low price.

You can save money by using smaller pieces of thinner wood

purchased in bulk, especially early on.

CHAPTER THREE
OTHER WOOD BURNING TOOLS

The Necessary Tools

The following tools are absolute necessities:

Tweezers or Pliers

Pliers will spare your precious little hands if you have a solid-point wood burning tool.

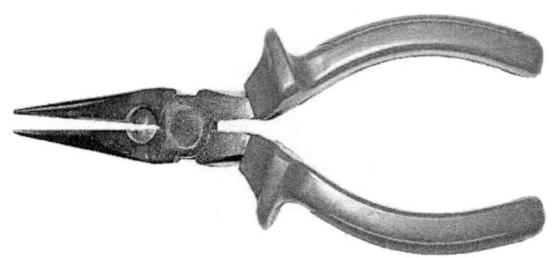

You don't have to wait for ages for the burner to cool down before switching points if you have a hot wood burning tool.

Simply turn off your burner for long enough to carefully twist the point out with your handy little pliers and replace it with a new point.

Chrome vanadium steel pliers are ideal. They're more durable and resistant to heat.

TIPS

I. To avoid cross-threading, begin by twisting the tip back in by hand. However, once it comes into touch with that hot burner, your point will quickly heat up. Snag your pliers, to save your fingers, and slowly twist that new point in till it's firm, but not too firmly, so you don't strip your wood-burning tool!

II. Pliers heat up as well, and quickly too, when used on a hot point. Therefore, keep a stone coaster handy to offer your hot pliers a place to rest when you're finished.

Tweezers, on the other hand, are used for wire-nib tools.

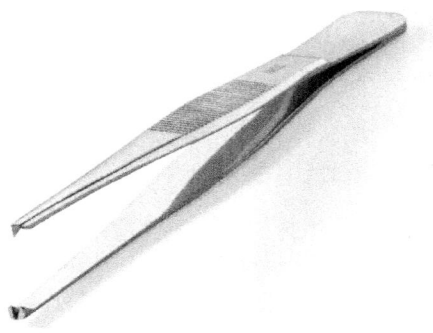

While wire-nibs cool down faster than solid-points, the base of the nib can sometimes retain enough heat to make pulling it out uncomfortable.

Simply turn off your machine, grasp the base of your nib with your tweezers, and carefully (, or not so gently) pull that hot little nib out of your pyrography pen.

After that, just replace the nib in your burning pen and you're good to go!

If you acquire your wire-nib wood burning tool as part of a kit, the tweezers are nearly always included.

If you buy the machine and pen separately, you'll have to hunt down the tweezers and add them to your cart.

Small Dish

What are you going to do with those hot points and nibs now that you've switched them?

If you do put them on your desk, you will undoubtedly regret it.

A dish is such a no-brainer answer in this case!

Plus, if you maintain those hot tips in a prominent location and move them out of the way properly, you avoid accidentally setting your arm down on one when you start burning again.

Dishes made of ceramic, porcelain, stone, clay, or metal that are heat resistant, are the ideal types to use.

Consider the following also: a trinket tray, jewelry dish, ring dish, a pretty flat dipping bowl, a tea cup saucer, etc.

TIP

Avoid going for bowls! The ideal dishes are small, flat, and have a lip. If you have more than one point in your dish, they won't immediately roll off onto your table, but they will also be easy to pluck out.

You can use a ring of hot glue to secure the bottom to prevent it from wobbling when you place the tips. It works flawlessly and looks fantastic on your studio table.

Sand Eraser (Ink Eraser)

Prior to burning, the majority of pyrographers sketch or trace a design onto the wood piece.

However, if you've ever tried to wipe graphite off wood, whether from a pencil or tracing paper, you'll understand why this is necessary.

Sandpaper doesn't appear to be fine enough to remove that rubbish. Even with a lot of elbow grease, a rubber art eraser isn't abrasive enough to really wipe those marks off the wood.

Certain ink erasers feature stronger rubber, which is beneficial to the ink!

The sand eraser, on the other hand, is the ideal tool for erasing those bothersome lines from your wood.

Bean Bags

These are used to raise your hand to the same height as the chunk of wood being burned.

At times, you may be working on a piece that is two inches thick and there is simply no appropriate place to rest your hands (this can be said to be artist cramp).

To level your hand with your wood, you can prop it up on your pinky. Your pinky, on the other hand, will undoubtedly protest after a while.

Other items, such as a box or another piece of wood, can be used to prop your hand up. These bean bags, however, are much easier to move around and conform to your hand perfectly wherever they are placed.

You can have up to four bean bags on hand, but you'll probably only need two.

Small Knife, Chisel, or Razor Blade

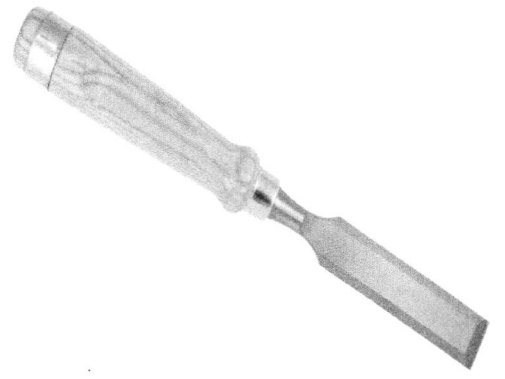

If you make a pyrography error, the wood may never forgive you.

All of it can be changed with one of these small tools and probably some sandpaper.

Scrape off dark burns to lighten them, or just add texture to your piece by bringing the natural wood back to the surface, with razors and small blades.

The chisel is the more severe tool. It's for serious business, and it's for grave errors.

Chisel deeply enough to blend out the dig site, and then blend in a fresh burn after smoothening out the dent with fine 220 grit sandpaper.

The Not-So-Necessary Tools
Sandpaper

This is used to clean up after you burn and to smooth your wood before you burn.

Burning a smooth piece of wood takes less effort. As a result, sand before each burn.

To remove the tough things, start with 80-grit. Then, for a buttery smooth surface, finish with a 220-grit. With finer sanding, your finishing sealant may not adhere.

This is also great for erasing minor mistakes or cleaning up any "glow" from a burn that you don't like.

Small knife, chisel, or razor blade are required for major errors.

CHAPTER FOUR

WOOD BURNING PROCEDURE

Preparing Your Wood

You should not attempt to start burning on a piece of wood until it has been properly prepared. You can create a smooth and level surface to work on by prepping your wood. This makes creating good lines a lot easier.

The only thing you have to do to prepare your wood is sand it down. Sand continuously until you get a smooth surface.

As you work, it is recommended that you gradually switch to a finer grit of sandpaper. As a result, each successive finer grit eliminates scratches from the previous grit.

If you think it will work better for your project, you can alter the grain during sanding. Keep in mind that burning with the grain is easier, so make sure the grain runs in the same direction as the majority of the lines in your pattern (, or design).

You can skip this step if you bought prepared wood from a hobby shop or craft store because it will already be smooth. There should also be no grain issues to be concerned about.

Selecting Your Design

Before you begin your wood-burning project, you must first select what you want to make (i.e., create). Pyrography designs can be downloaded for free or purchased.

Free Pyrography Designs

These websites provide free and printable designs for woodburning:

- ✓ Homesthetics (https://homesthetics.net/epic-free-printable-wood-burning-patterns/) – offers 28+ designs
- ✓ Mostcraft (https://www.mostcraft.co

m/free-printable-wood-burning-patterns/) – offers 22 designs
- ✓ GuidePatterns (https://www.guidepatterns.com/27-free-wood-burning-pattern-ideas.php) offers 27 designs

Books with pyrography designs can also be purchased.

It's also possible to make your own patterns. If you are skilled in this area, you can draw them freehand. You can make them on a computer or copy a picture to use as a template (, or design).

You'll print these designs or remove them from the pattern

book, then transfer them to the wood with graphite or carbon paper.

Here are the actions you'll take to accomplish this:

1. Graphite or carbon paper should be taped to your wood.

2. Next, tape on top of the graphite paper, the design paper.

3. Trace, firmly, the lines of the design with a pen or tool.

4. Take away both papers.

HINT: *The graphite paper has two sides, one darker, and one lighter. The graphite will be* *transferred onto the wood if the darker side is facing the wood.*

Don't be scared to push down, because to transfer the design, you'll need to apply slight pressure. However, be cautious when selecting a tool because you don't want something sharp to shred (, or tear) the paper, making the tracing procedure more difficult or damaging the wood.

Stencils, like those used in other crafts, are another choice for producing your design. You'll need to use a standard pencil to trace the stencil onto your wood. It's not a good idea to try to hold the stencil and burn it. This may cause the stencil to become damaged, as well as burns on your hands.

When it comes to your first design, keep it simple and straightforward. Because black and white designs do not require shading, which is a more advanced skill, they are the best. Additionally, ensure that the pattern's size is the right size for your wood piece.

Burning Your Design

You're ready to start burning now that you have all of your supplies and have chosen, prepped, and transferred a design onto your wood. Turn on your wood burner and, adjust it to the appropriate temperature if it has a temperature control.

The temperature setting you use will be determined by the sort of wood you're using. Harder wood demands more heat, while soft wood requires less. You'll have to experiment to see what works best, since the exact temperature setting required varies according to the wood burner you're using.

You should practice on a scrap piece of wood before starting on your project. You can put the temperature setting to the test. This will also allow you to get a feel for how the wood burner works, allowing you to experiment with the speed at which you move the pen and the amount of pressure you use.

It also provides you with the opportunity to make mistakes. Making a mistake or doing something incorrectly on a scrap piece of wood is preferable to doing it on your project piece.

Tracing the lines in the design is the first step once you're ready to start your project. You just want to go over all of the lines at this point. If your design has shade, there is no need to worry about filling in or adding shading.

You want to slowly guide the pen across the wood while holding it firmly. For the best results, keep your hand steady and moving. The darker and deeper a spot becomes, the longer the wood burner is held in that spot. Going slowly will help you prevent gouges, deep grooves, and lines that are too thick or too dark, since you want your lines to be smooth and even.

You can start filling in and adding shading and other features, after you've traced all of the lines. Maintain a steady hand, and work slowly once more.

Adding Color to Your Art

Once you've mastered wood burning, you might want to

experiment with adding color to your pyrography artwork. You can do this with watercolor pencils, wax-based oil pencils or crayons, gel paints, or wood gel stains, among other art products. Regular wood paint can also be used; however, it may be more difficult to handle as a novice.

Finishing Your Pyrography Art

You can use sandpaper to smooth out some of the rough spots after you've completed burning your design into the wood. Any lingering wood residue on the artwork can also be wiped off with a soft cloth.

To give the wood a great shine, you can use mineral oil or olive oil. Lacquer or shellac can be used to provide the look of lacquered wood.

Tips on Making Your First Project Successful

You've learned the fundamentals of how to begin your first wood-burning project. Now is the time to learn a few pointers and tactics that will help you improve your skills in this area.

Tips on the Tips

Now that you know how vital the tips on your wood burner are, you can see why it's so important to keep them in good shape. While working, wipe your tips off as needed, and always clean them after completing a project.

When you notice a black build-up on your tip, you know it's time to clean it. Carbon is a natural byproduct of burning wood, and it causes this build-up. Turning up the heat on the wood burner to try to burn it off is a no-go area, since this may cause the tips to wear out faster.

When you remove your tips from the wood burner, allow them to cool completely in a fireproof dish before storing them in a box or somewhere secure to avoid bending, cracking, or breaking them. To avoid burns, always use pliers to remove and replace tips on a hot tool.

Due to the fact that old tips get hotter, it's also worth noting that a new tip requires a higher temperature than an old tip.

Tips While You're Working

Always keep safety in mind when working on a project. The tool's end and tips get incredibly hot. The temperature can reach hundreds of degrees. Make sure the end isn't touching or leaning against anything that could catch fire.

Always work on a fire-resistant surface and observe all of the safety precautions included with your wood-burning pen. Consider installing a small fan in your workspace to assist in the removal of smoke while you work. This will assist you in avoiding irritation of the lungs. If your pen is smoking excessively, it is too hot, and you should switch it off and wait for it to cool down or lower the temperature.

One thing to keep in mind while picking wood is to stay away from pine. While it is a soft wood with a good appearance, it contains a lot of resin. When heated, this can cause bubbles and stickiness on your work surface and wood burner.

Always use a standard (, or regular) pencil when drawing your designs on the wood. This makes erasing lines easier, and it also burns up as you work. Since colored pencils contain wax, which can melt when you burn over the lines; they are a no-go area.

You should use a white artist's eraser, when it comes to the eraser. Normal pink erasers can sometimes leave a residue on your wood that stains it.

Getting two pieces of wood and using one of them as your practice canvas, as described above, is a terrific idea for any project. If you don't want to do this for every project, at the very least do it whenever you work with a new type of wood or new tips, because changes in your tools and supplies will demand you to adjust how you work.

Tips for Finishing the Piece

After completion, you can stain or paint your project to give it a more finished look. You can do this instead of shading if you wish to paint your project. Burn the outline of your design but leave the inside areas unburned so they can be painted.

CHAPTER FIVE
PYROGRAPHY STENCILS

The appropriate pyrography stencil is the foundation of any effective wood burning project. While you may be familiar with stencils used in a variety of other arts and crafts projects, the stencils used in wood burning are slightly different.

A pyrography stencil, unlike what you might think of when you hear the word "stencil," is more of a pattern than a tool.

What are the materials used to make pyrography stencils? By tracing an image onto a piece of wood, you can make a pyrography stencil. A variety of materials, including graphite paper, carbon paper, metal, and even plastic, can be used to create the stencil.

Wood burning is a craft that is both calming and fascinating. You'll almost certainly want to start your design off with a stencil, whether you wish to do it as a hobby or as a business.

If you want to get proficient at pyrography, you'll need to learn a lot about making and using stencils.

Premade Stencils

You can draw images and designs directly onto the wood, but this takes time, especially if you want to transfer a complex image or design, if you don't want to use a stencil. Using a pre-made physical stencil is significantly easier.

A premade physical stencil can be produced out of a variety of materials. Plastic and metal are the most frequent. You'll need to trace the stencil onto your wood if you use this type of stencil. You can do this with a standard pencil.

HINT: *Unlike other crafts, such as painting, do not try to hold the stencil and burn the wood at the same time. This is harmful and can result in burns. It's also possible that the stencil will be damaged.*

You may order or customize a variety of metal and plastic stencils. If you're not sure whether to go with metal or plastic, here's a comparison of both:

- ✓ While metal stencils are expensive, plastic stencils are priced reasonably.
- ✓ Metal stencils are heavy, while plastic stencils are light.
- ✓ While metal stencils are difficult to store, plastic stencils are easy to store.
- ✓ Metal stencils are not as simple to locate; plastic stencils are easily accessible.

- ✓ Metal stencils are not as customizable, but plastic stencils are.

The number of physical stencils available is nearly limitless. Metal stencils are most commonly used to create letters, but they can also be used to create a variety of other designs. Customization options are more likely to be available with plastic stencils.

Graphite Paper

Another option is to make your own stencil out of graphite paper. This is nothing more than a traced pattern, essentially. You'll use graphite paper to transfer the stencil, a printed design, to the board.

If you don't want to deal with a physical stencil owing to storage concerns or other personal preferences, this is an excellent alternative. It also allows you to be more inventive with your designs.

One side of the graphite paper you'll use is coated with graphite, which when pressed against the wood will transfer your pattern. This side is darker than the other, making it easy to distinguish between them. To make your stencil, you'll only need a few tools:

- ✓ Graphite paper
- ✓ Stylus or tracing tool
- ✓ Pattern or design on plain paper

You are going to start out with graphite paper. The dark side or transfer side should be laid directly on your wood piece. Use a couple of strips of tape to keep it in place and prevent it from slipping.

Next, you'll need a pattern or design printed on normal (regular) paper. Place this piece of paper on top of the graphite paper and tape it in place.

Ensure that tape that won't tear the papers or harm the wood is used, such as masking tape. It only needs to keep the papers in place, preventing them from shifting as you work.

Tracing the design or pattern is the next step. You can do this with almost anything, but ensure the tip is dull. Because you'll need to apply some pressure to ensure the graphite transfers to the wood, a sharp point will tear the paper. Trace over every line and detail in your pattern or design with your tool.

Remove the papers once you've finished tracing and start woodburning.

Carbon Paper

You might be wondering if you can substitute carbon paper for graphite. You certainly can, but carbon isn't the finest option for wood. Below is a comparison of the two options, and explains why graphite is the best option.

- ✓ Graphite is erasable, but carbon is difficult to erase
- ✓ While graphite is cleaner to work with, carbon can stain wood.
- ✓ With graphite, you get clearer transfer, whereas, carbon smears easily

- ✓ While graphite leaves no residue, carbon leaves ink residue

As you can see, carbon is a messier alternative that may damage your wood and make creating a clean final project more challenging. Because it is made of the same material as a pencil lead, graphite is considerably easier to work with.

When working with it, you have more control and precision. It's also simple to clean, in addition.

You may, of course, use carbon if you choose. It is less expensive and easier to come by than graphite paper. Numerous woodburning enthusiasts have no problems with it.

Graphite, on the other hand, is considered to be easier to work with as a novice.

Patterns and Designs Selection

You'll want to exercise caution when you're looking for patterns, designs, and physical stencils to use in your woodworking. There are two things to remember in general:

- ✓ Your level of expertise
- ✓ The wood

Always select a design concept that is appropriate for your skill level. If you're new to the trade, look for designs that are simpler and less detailed. Anything requiring delicate details, like fine lines or a great deal of shading should be left to more experienced woodworkers.

HINT: *Sticking to projects that are appropriate for your skill level keeps you motivated and allows you to see early results. That will spur you on to keep going!*

You should also consider the size and type of wood you'll use for your project. You'll want to choose a pattern that fits the wood nicely, in general.

It should allow enough space around the object for a bare edge, but not too much. In any case, you don't want to end up with a pattern that's much too large or small for your wood.

Occasionally, the wood you wish to use will provide inspiration. A piece that appears to have water ripples on it is a good example, as it may inspire you to create some sort of water scene.

Allow your wood to speak to you, and give you design suggestions.

A stencil can be made out of nearly anything. Photographs of people, animals, and places are included. You can use these to make realistic graphics in your woodworking projects.

The hardest aspect of pyrography is generally deciding what to create. Choose a design, image, or pattern with care. You should be fine as long as you make sure that anything you choose is appropriate for your skill level and wood.

Start Working on Your Project

When learning pyrography, one of the first things you'll do is learn how to make a pyrography stencil. You must ensure that you comprehend the procedure in order to transfer patterns and designs more easily.

Fortunately, learning how to do it with graphite paper is very simple. Assemble your materials, choose a pattern or design, and start making your first pyrography stencil.

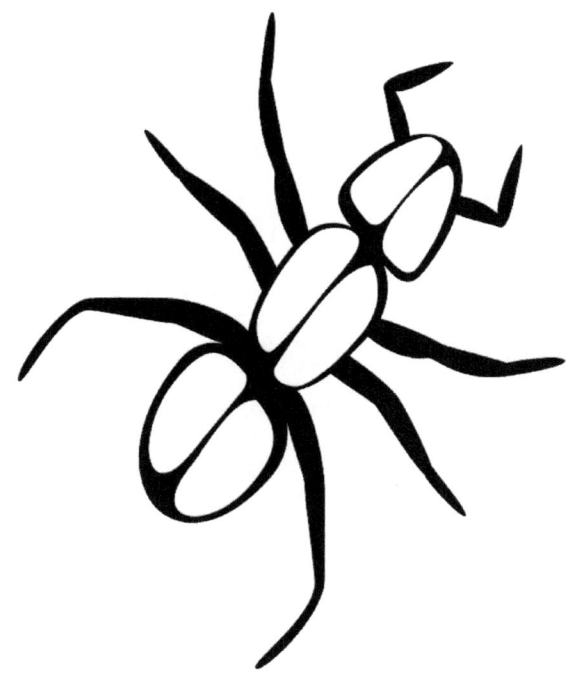

CHAPTER SIX

TECHNIQUES AND TRICKS

Basic Outlines

This section will be quite familiar if you've ever done any line art using a pen.

Trick: *Using sure traces, and going slowly, try to do it in one stroke. Try moving both your hands and the piece of wood for a softer movement, if you are making large curves. Avoid hushing, or you risk scratching the wood rather than burning it.*

For being sharp enough to lift the wood around the trace, this tip leaves little walls flanking each line. This texture is really stunning. You have more movement freedom and may quickly adjust the direction of your traces with a circular tip that does not sink into the wood.

Filling Silhouettes (Technique)
It's always easier to fill in black than it is to make gradients, and it can look just as nice. A flat gradient tip with medium to high heat is recommended for large surfaces. The calligraphy pen is fantastic for little areas.

Trick: *If you don't want to leave unsightly (, or ugly) stroke marks all over your drawing, don't try to fill it with as much heat as possible. Working on a medium heat setting with soft circular motions, darken each area at a time slowly.*

Special Trick: *When you first touch the wood, gently blow on your tip, and let it heat up naturally as you travel in a short circular motion. This will ensure a successful start!*

The more heat you use, the opaque the outcome will be. Create contrasts against shiny gradients using this concept.

Gradient Effect (Technique)

Gradients are more difficult to create than black fills since they require less heat, more patience, and finer control.

For this job, always use a flat tip and a wood burner with temperature control. A temperature range of 4 to 5/10 is sufficient for most woods.

Start slowly with circular movements and heat up one small area at a time in this situation. You won't notice any difference at first, but the shading will gradually appear. Because neighboring (, or adjacent) areas are already warm, it is always easier to move along them rather than back and forth between distant areas of the surface.

Significant: Take care with wood grains, as you won't be able to burn as efficiently in these areas. Gradients will be considerably tougher to see if the grains are large. More heat can always be applied to these locations.

Hatching (Technique)

Hatching and cross-hatching may give you a lovely shading and texture look without the hassle of producing gradients, and if your wood is too grainy, they may even work better.

Use a tracing tip (such as the spear-shaped one) as if you were drawing any other line, for this technique. Begin by hatching in one direction, always beginning at the edges; this will cause the stroke to burn stronger in the outline, and progressively weaker in the drawing's interior (i.e., inside).

Try some cross-hatching by adding another set of lines perpendicular to the first to make your shading truly pop.

Textures (Technique)

There are an endless number of textures you may imitate by burning, so here are a few tips:

Hair: Use the flat shading tip with a higher heat intensity for wild hairstyles reminiscent of the 1980's or to create a little sloppy look. You don't need to be smooth this time since you want to leave direction markings all over the place. You can vary between dark black strokes and softer shades by controlling the pressure you apply. To make things easier, start by outlining the hair volume and defining the lighting blank places.

Fur: A tracing point, either sharp or round, can be used to create an amazing appearance of short, soft fur while also accounting for shading. The golden rule is to use more heat and closer strokes in regions that you want to appear darker, and less heat and faster strokes in areas that you want to appear lighter. Smooth your lines with a flat shading tip if you think the overall look is too sharp.

Scales or Leathery Skin: To simulate cracked skin, sharp and fractured lines are applied. For shading, use a flat tip and then, create volume by making the edges very dark. If you don't want to end up with a furry dragon, don't employ hatching in this situation.

Background Techniques

When you've completed your main burning, it's time to consider the background. It can make a significant difference in how your project looks overall, particularly if you make use of a cheap-looking piece of wood. The approaches listed here are appropriate for any degree of work or time you plan to devote to this tedious step.

Rust: When you don't have much time to waste, this is by far the simplest technique. You can take a few corroded nuts and bolts and use sandpaper to remove some of the rust. Simply pick up some of the dust with your fingertips and spread it across the surface just like you would with chalk or charcoal, to use on the wood. Use a cotton ball instead of your fingers if you don't want reddish fingers.

This technique produces a rust covering that is smooth and opaque when used on MDF (Medium-Density Fiberboard). When the main burning has a glossy gradient, it is highly intriguing to make the background opaque so that it stands out.

Heat blower: Frequently the best option for the majority, a heat blower can be used to create an excellent vignette effect. Turn on the blower, and never blow in the same location for more than a second, work your way around the edges. Heat the entire area by moving around it and heating it evenly. It will take some time before you begin to notice shading, but once it does, the process is pretty rapid (i.e., in the blink of an eye, it will get darker and darker).

Make sure the metal tip of the heat blower does not come into contact with the wood or your skin. You may wind up with a significant scar as a result of an accident.

Shading or filling: You can try gradient filling or even go completely black, if you have enough patience or don't have any large regions to fill. The whole black background is sometimes required for the art, although this is an enormous amount of work.

Therefore, proceed only if you are convinced that the end result will be worthwhile; otherwise, the background will cause you more headaches than the actual work.

Dotting: This is an extremely ancient technique that may be found in several medieval art pieces; it was done at the time by heating metal bolts and "branding" the wood with them multiple times. For this type of work, even the cheapest wood burners will now come with a large round tip. Fill the backdrop one dot at a time, stopping to clean the tip anytime it gathers too much matter, once the burner is really hot. This results in a true bevel edge as well as the shiny/opaque contrast, when done in a softwood.

CHAPTER SEVEN
CLEANING PYROGRAPHY TOOL TIPS

The accumulation of carbon is inconvenient.

Carbon is the black substance that appears on the tips while you burn, if you're unfamiliar with the term.

You'll have to keep turning up the heat on your machine to create the same burn, since heat has a difficult time penetrating it.

When carbon buildup breaks free from your tip, it makes a mess all over your artwork, leaving marks when you attempt to wipe it away.

However, if you clean your tool, you'll be back in business in no time.

The Most Effective Cleaning Methods

Solid-point burners, tips, and points are more durable (, or sturdy) than wire-nibs, which means they may occasionally withstand more abuse.

A heated tip, on the other hand, is still soft and flexible (, or malleable).

To put it another way, you must still use caution.

Leather Strop and Aluminum Oxide

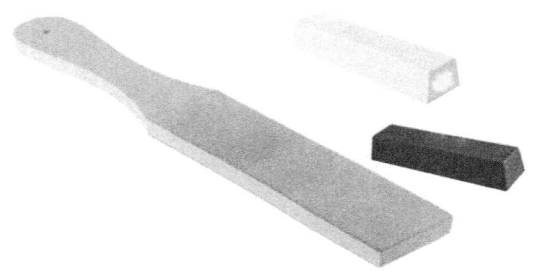

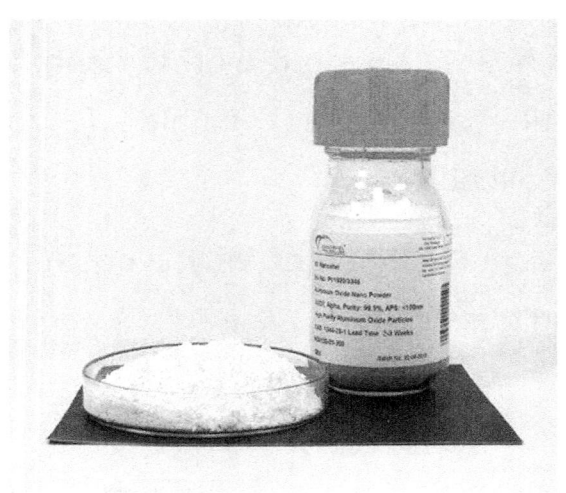

This is recommended for all tip styles.

A leather strop has a rougher leather strip on one side (which is the inside of the skin) and a smoother leather strip on the other (which is the outside of the skin).

The grit that scrubs off the carbon is aluminum oxide.

Powdered aluminum oxide should be used instead of wax polishing compound. When you first get your tip hot, the wax leaves a slight sticky residue that smells. The powder, on the other hand, does not.

How to Use:

On the rough side of your leather strop, apply a small amount of powder (alternatively, rub the wax). Then rub the strop with the cool tip until it is clean. To acquire a *sparkly* finish on those tips, flip the leather strop over to the smooth side and rub again.

Honing Cleaning Cloth

This is also recommended for all tip styles.

With a honing cloth, you can get a good cleaning. It doesn't produce the same brilliant shine as a leather strop, but it's less expensive and still effective.

It cleans in a similar fashion to fine sand paper, but it doesn't leave those horrible scrape lines (, or marks) and damage on your tips.

How to Use:

Rub your honing cloth over the dirty areas of the tip until it shines like new, or near enough.

Acceptable Cleaning Methods

These cleaning methods are popular among certain pyrographers. At the very least, these methods shouldn't harm your pyrography tools.

Razor Blade or Knife

This cleaning method can be used for straight edge or flat tip styles.

It is, however, not good for rounded tips.

A cleaning tool with knives attached is available from certain brands, and are well-liked by many persons.

These instruments, however, do not work well with rounded tips such as ballpoints or flow tips.

How to Use:

Scrape your tip across the blade's edge gently until the carbon comes off.

If you can fasten the razor blade or knife to something sturdy, such as a 2 x 4 piece of wood, that is preferable. The carbon can then be scraped off easily without the need to stabilize both the blade and the tip.

Brass Bristled Brush

This cleaning method can be used for all solid-point tip styles.

It's a little scratchy for the sleeker wire-nibs, but it's adequate for solid-point tips.

Simply ensure that the bristles of the brush are soft brass, not a stainless-steel brush, which is harsh and tough.

How to Use:

Simply rub along the brass bristles, the solid-point tips, until all carbon has been removed.

Steel Wool or Scouring Pad

You can use this for all solid-point tip styles.

Another method for cleaning your solid-point tips that is both wonderful and inexpensive. The scouring pads are a little too abrasive for the wire-nibs, on the one hand.

With these, you can scrape that bothersome carbon off your solid-point tips quickly and easily.

How to Use:

Simply rub the tip against the pad until the carbon is removed. You can twist the tip of the rounded tips to clean them better.

Tea Strainer

This cleaning method can be used for all tip styles.

The tea strainer is revered by some. Other pyrographers have reported that it has damaged their tools.

You may find it repulsive, and you'd be lucky if you got a thorough cleaning once in a while. It does, however, remove large carbon chunks, and you may use it from time to time.

If you're going to be using it, the best strainers are the finer ones, not the coarser ones.

How to Use:

Rub the dirty tip gently against the tea strainer mesh until the carbon is removed.

Awful Cleaning Methods

These should not be used even if you already have them on hand, as you may be thinking right now.

Your tips will wear out quickly, and your tools will be ruined by these ones.

Just keep in mind that while these methods WILL clean your tips, they WILL wear them out faster and can easily destroy them.

Sandpaper and Sanding Blocks

Many people are guilty of cleaning their pyrography tools with sandpaper.

While the tips clean up quickly, they scratch easily, especially the more expensive wire-nibs.

Please avoid using something as nasty as 80-grit, if you're going to use it! Something fine such as 220-grit, or even 1500+ grit, should be used instead.

However, let me reiterate: sand paper is not a good idea.

Emery Boards and Files

Sandpaper is even better compared to these: they are simply worse!

On your pyrography tool, never use emery boards or nail files.

Wet Sponge

Rust is a dreadful substance.

Although a lot of persons use it, because it's one of the most popular ways to clean a soldering iron, it is not healthy for the metal.

Furthermore, it does not perform as well as other procedures in removing that stubborn carbon.

CHAPTER EIGHT
PYROGRAPHY SAFETY GEAR, TIPS AND TRICKS

Safety Tools and Gear

These woodburning tools and safety equipment can help you avoid injuring yourself or causing long-term harm.

The importance of safety cannot be overstated.

In the world of pyrography, heat, smoke, and toxic woods are all genuine dangers. Do not fall prey to them.

1. **Adjustable drawing table:** This is very useful at assisting in keeping heat away from fingers and face.

Additionally, it aids in artist posture.

2. Keep fingers from getting too hot with **leather gloves, rubber finger guards, finger heat shields, or thick cork grips**. As for the leather gloves, you can go for thinner options, which allow for easy movement of fingers. But then, you'll have to use it in combination with one of the other tools, such as the rubber finger guards.

3. **P95 Mask:** This is used to protect the lungs from smoke and sanding.

4. **Fan:** This assists in moving smoke and heat away from your face and fingers. Even better, invest in a fan with an activated charcoal filter that will filter smoke from the air as it is drawn away from you.

5. **Air purifier:** Removes smoke and particles from the air caused by burning and sanding.

Safety Tips and Tricks

1. Avoid touching the metal while the machine is running!

2. Burners should be kept away from combustible materials.

3. Jewelry, loose hanging hair, headphones, etc. should be tied back.

4. It is recommended that you work on a hard, sturdy surface, like a table or desk. There's no need to burn holes in your couch or, for that matter, your leg.

5. It is critical that you secure the stand to a table. This way, you also avoid ending up with holes in your carpet.

6. When not in use, always put your burner on the stand.

7. When you leave the table, turn off the burner. When

you leave the room, unplug the burner.

8. Gently remove hot tips or insert cold tips into a hot burner using metal pliers. To cool, place the hot tips in a heat-safe dish. Stop, back up, and try again if a tip refuses to go in.

9. Only use non-toxic, dry, well-seasoned wood that has not been chemically treated for burning. If you're burning something other than wood, such as fabric, bone, or cork, ensure they are devoid of chemical treatments, glues, stains, finishes, and so on.

10. Teach children how to be safe around pyrography tools. Keep hot tools away from them.

Worst Woods for Pyrography
Green Wood

This contains lots of sap and water, which produces much smoke, and also slows down burning.

Water makes the wood more resistant to fire, whereas sap gums up your tips and accomplishes the same terrible thing water does.

Certain types of tree sap can also cause severe allergy reactions in certain persons.

Driftwood

When sea salt is burned, the chlorine in it transforms into cancer-causing nastiness.

This salt can be found in sea-soaked driftwood.

This one should be avoided at all costs.

Chemically Treated Wood

Anything with a finish or glue, whether painted, stained, or sealed, should be avoided for burning.

The fumes that these emit usually give you headaches or make you feel strange.

Wood pallets, plywood, and chipboard, are other items that people frequently burn but should never be burned.

All of them have been chemically treated.

Keep a safe distance from them.

Poisonous Woods

When wood with natural poisons is burned, hazardous fumes are produced, and the poisons are occasionally disseminated into the air.

Here are a few examples:

- ✓ Mexican Elder
- ✓ Oleander
- ✓ Mexican Pepper

Also, avoid burning for pyrography, any wood with the word "poison" in the name, such as poison ivy, poison sumac, or poison oak.

Smoky Woods

This is an ambiguous area.

In the wood burning community, several woods that are fairly popular include smoky woods such as:

- ✓ Pine
- ✓ Fir
- ✓ Cypress

While they are really popular, you do not want to inhale the smoke.

When burning smokey woods, make sure you're wearing your P95 safety mask and using all of the appropriate safety equipment.

Best woods for Pyrography
- ✓ Willow
- ✓ Aspen
- ✓ Basswood
- ✓ Maple
- ✓ Cherry
- ✓ Poplar
- ✓ Birch
- ✓ Walnut
- ✓ Ash
- ✓ Pine

The following are some good runners-up with which ash or pine may be replaced:

- ✓ Beech (outside of cutting boards and wood spoons, it is difficult to find)
- ✓ Pecan
- ✓ Sycamore
- ✓ Cedar
- ✓ Cork (avoid cork with glue)

CHAPTER NINE

BEGINNER SAMPLE PATTERNS

CHAPTER TEN

IN CONCLUSION

Pyrography is a beautiful term for this craft because it signifies "fire writing." For centuries, people have used this technique to adorn wood and a variety of other materials, including leather and clay.

Historically, they were used to embellish or customize items in order to identify who owned them. However, with the tools that are currently available, you will be able to express yourself much more artistically.

Wood burning is a fantastic hobby for those who enjoy working with organic materials to create art. A wood burning kit, which includes a wood burning tool, tips, and a few other useful tools, is available for beginners. Small wooden slices can also be found at your local craft store or online to practice with.

A wood burning tool can be used to adorn a limitless number of items. Numerous individuals enjoy wood burning things such as culinary utensils (spoons, chopping boards, etc.), home decor, and jewelry.

You can begin your first project now that you understand the fundamentals of wood-burning. To show off your fire writing skills, find the correct piece of wood and the right pattern.

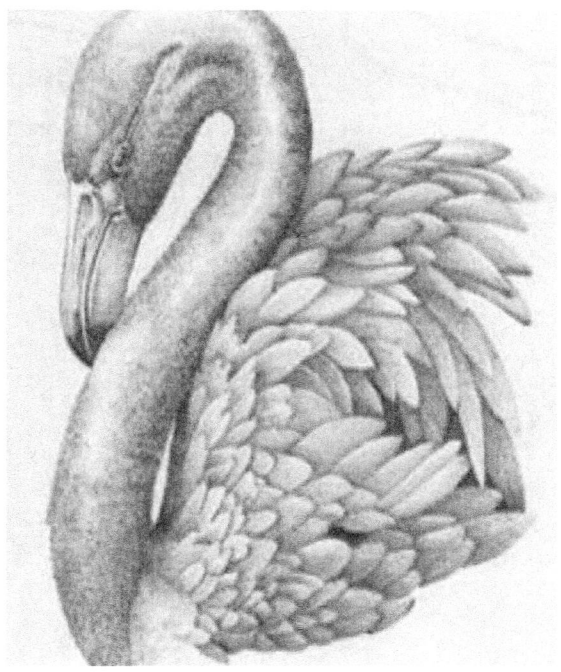

Printed in Great Britain
by Amazon

18668274R00078